W9-CMC-257

Contents

Confederate and Union States in 1861

Legend:
- □ Capital cities
- Union States
- Confederate States
- Seceded from Virginia
- Border States
- United States Territories

While the Confederate states covered about as much territory as the Union states, they held fewer people, fewer factories, and fewer railroad tracks and locomotives. These would be significant drawbacks for the Confederacy during the Civil War. The South would also lose part of its support when West Virginia separated from the rest of Virginia in 1863.

The War between the States

The Civil War was fought between 1861 and 1865. It was the bloodiest conflict in United States history, with more soldiers killed and wounded than in any other war. It was also a pivotal event in U.S. history: It transformed the lives of millions of African-American men, women, and children by freeing them from slavery. It also transformed the nation, changing it from a loose confederation of states into a powerful country with a strong central government.

On one side were eleven southern states that had split from the United States to form a new country, the Confederate States of America, led by President Jefferson Davis. They took this step after Abraham Lincoln was elected president of the United

States in 1860. Southerners feared Lincoln would end slavery, which was central to their economy and society. The northern states, or the **Union**, declared this split illegal.

A big question was whether the four **Border States** (Delaware, Maryland, Kentucky, and Missouri) would join the **Confederacy**. They had slavery, too, but they also held many people loyal to the Union. To keep control of these states, Lincoln felt early in the war that he could not risk moving against slavery, fearing that to do so would drive the Border States out of the Union. Later, however, he did declare the emancipation, or freedom, of Southern slaves.

In the Border States, and in many others, families divided sharply, with some men fighting for one side and some for the other. The Civil War has been called a war of "brother against brother."

Fighting broke out on April 12, 1861, when gunners for the South began shelling Union soldiers in Fort Sumter in Charleston Harbor, South Carolina. This attack led Lincoln to call for troops to put down what he called an armed rebellion. Thousands of Northerners flocked to the Union army. Thousands of Southerners joined the Confederate army, determined to win independence for their side.

Soldiers in both the Union and Confederate armies suffered the hardships—and occasional boredom—of life in an army camp. They also fought in huge battles with great bravery and heroism. At times, both sides treated their enemies with honor and respect. At other times, they treated them with cruelty and brutality.

The opposing armies fought in two main areas, or theaters. The eastern theater included Pennsylvania, Virginia, and Maryland; the region near the Confederate capital of Richmond, Virginia; and the Union capital of Washington, D.C. The huge western theater stretched from eastern Kentucky and Tennessee down to the Gulf of Mexico and all the way to New Mexico. By the end of the many bloody battles across these lands, the Union won in 1865, and the states reunited into a single country.

The Civil War was a turning point in U.S. history. Before the war, the North and South had competed politically and economically. The war left the South much weaker and the North much stronger. More importantly, the war ended decades of arguments over slavery. While the war made African Americans free, however, what that freedom would mean for them—and the rest of the country—was not clear.

CHAPTER ONE

The Cost of the War

*"Of the thousand
officers and men who started out with us
four hundred and seventy-four were not with us now.
. . . From those who have lived to return come no words of
regret. . . . What matters the loss of all these years? What matters the trial, the sickness, the wounds! What we went out to do
is done. The war is ended, and the Union is saved!"*

Ted Upson, former Union soldier from Indiana, 1884

The Dead

The Civil War exacted a terrible human cost. About 680,000 soldiers and sailors lost their lives. In fact, more Americans died in this war than in any other U.S. conflict. Only World War II, with almost 410,000 deaths, even comes close.

Of course, these numbers do not include civilian deaths. The exact number of civilian deaths is not known, however.

The Wounded

Nearly half a million more men were wounded. More than twenty thousand

These graves at the Union military base in City Point, Virginia, hold both Union and Confederate dead. Army camps and prisoner-of-war camps needed cemeteries to hold the tens of thousands of soldiers who died of disease as well as their wounds.

ENORMOUS SACRIFICES

In this chart, the right columns for the Union and for the Confederacy show the total of the wounded and the dead, plus the grand total. The left columns hold a breakdown of the dead into four categories, each covering a cause of death.

Civil War Casualties

	UNION		CONFEDERATE*	
Wounded, not fatally		277,401		194,000
DEATHS				
Killed in battle, including fatal wounds	111,904		94,000	
Died of disease	227,580		164,000	
Died in prison	30,192		26,000–31,000	
Died from other causes	24,881		Unknown	
TOTAL DEATHS		394,557		287,000
TOTAL CASUALTIES		**671,958**		**481,000**

* Estimates; official figures are not reliable.

Northerners—and an unknown number of Southerners—had undergone **amputations**. Some of these men found it difficult to adjust to civilian life. A few thousand soldiers were placed in mental hospitals, but the war's emotional impact also showed in many other veterans' behavior.

Many veterans, of course, did return to normal life, though they needed time to adjust. Some looked back on their service as a positive experience. Oliver Wendell Holmes Jr. saw the war as a test of the soldiers' spirits, an experience that helped make them strong.

A Shattered Land

Union soldiers went home to bustling cities and thriving farms. Confederate soldiers returned to a South badly damaged by war. Many cities were in ruins. About two-thirds of all railroad tracks had been pulled up. Farms had been destroyed and forests cut down. In many areas, homes had been burned to the ground or looted. Confederate money and **bonds** were worth nothing. The wealth many Southerners had once enjoyed was gone because much of it was based on the value of enslaved people who were now free.

OLIVER WENDELL HOLMES JR.

Oliver Wendell Holmes Jr. was born to a prominent Boston family in 1841. He graduated from Harvard College in Massachusetts in 1861 and joined the Union army. During his three years of service, he was wounded three times, twice almost fatally. After leaving the army, he went to Harvard Law School. Upon graduation, he began practicing law.

In 1882, Holmes was named to the state supreme court of Massachusetts, serving for twenty years, until he was named to the U.S. Supreme Court, where he remained until 1932. He is regarded as one of the greatest justices in the Court's history; he wrote opinions that clearly defined the principles of U.S. law. Many of those eloquent opinions were written against the majority ruling of the Court, gaining him the nickname "The Great Dissenter." Holmes died in 1935.

Peace or Revenge?

Some people in both the North and the South were ready to make peace with the people of the opposing side. Many, however, felt bitterness. Even the Southerners who accepted the South's defeat sometimes resented the attitude of Northerners.

Many Northerners wanted revenge on the South for causing the war. Congressman George Julian, a representative from Indiana, urged the nation to hang Confederate president Jefferson Davis and General Robert E. Lee for treason. "And stop there? Not at all," he continued. "I would hang liberally while I had my hands in."

"We are down . . . but, although defenseless, we don't like to be kicked and cuffed, belabored and berated. . . . The best thing that [Northerners] can do is to change the tone of [their] radical press and people, cease to call us ugly names . . . and instead of harsh [titles] and blows, extend a helping hand to us in our misfortunes."

Republican Vindicator, a newspaper in Staunton, Virginia, 1866

Massive fires left Richmond, Virginia, largely in ruins. The same was true in many other Southern cities.

THE LOST CAUSE

Southern whites had been confident that they would win the war and needed some explanation for why they had lost. They found it in a belief in the "Lost Cause," an interpretation of the Civil War that cast the Southerners' actions in a positive light. According to this belief, **seceding** from the Union had been just, but overwhelming Northern power had defeated the South. Some also blamed poor leadership by Jefferson Davis for the Confederacy's defeat.

The myth of the Lost Cause ignored the issue of slavery—the question of whether one people has the right to enslave another. It also glorified certain figures—especially Confederate generals Robert E. Lee and Thomas "Stonewall" Jackson—and honored the Southern soldier as a romantic warrior.

The Lost Cause shaped how many Southerners viewed their history for many decades. Some of these attitudes affected other Americans' view of the war as well; even outside the South, Lee was often considered a hero.

CHAPTER TWO

President Lincoln's Reconstruction

~

President Lincoln clashed with leaders in Congress over the issue of how to bring the Southern states back into the Union and how to treat former Confederates.

Posing the Questions

The great question that faced the nation in 1865 was how to treat the South. Should the states be accepted back into the Union? Should Confederate soldiers and government officials be allowed to vote and hold office? How should the freed African Americans be treated?

These questions formed the basis of a great debate in the North that had begun during the war. As Union troops gained control of parts of the South, the government needed a plan for **Reconstruction** with answers to those questions.

Lincoln's Policy

President Abraham Lincoln put forward such a plan. He did not hate or want to punish Southerners. He simply wanted to make sure that slavery was ended and that the most prominent Confederates were kept out of new Southern state governments.

Lincoln outlined his views late in 1863. He offered an **amnesty**, or freedom from prosecution, to most Southerners. They only had to swear an oath of loyalty to the United States. Lincoln did say that members of the Confederate government and top-ranking army officers would not be pardoned and might be prosecuted.

He also offered a plan for forming new state governments. The number of people in each state taking the oath was compared to the number of

*"I . . . proclaim . . . that a full **pardon** is hereby granted to them and each of them, with restoration of all rights of property, except as to slaves . . . [who] shall take and subscribe an oath . . . [swearing] to faithfully support, protect and defend the Constitution of the United States."*

Abraham Lincoln, Proclamation of Amnesty and Reconstruction, December 8, 1863

people in that state who had voted in the presidential election of 1860. Once 10 percent of the number of 1860 voters took the oath, they could form a new state government.

By taking the loyalty oath, Southerners promised to accept national laws about slavery. By late 1863, of course, Lincoln had issued the Emancipation Proclamation, freeing slaves in the Confederate states. In this way, Lincoln made sure that the new state governments in the South would end slavery.

Early in 1864, Louisiana formed a new state government, though not quite following the 10-percent plan. Later that year, a convention met to write a new **constitution** for the state. It ended slavery and granted many **civil rights** to blacks—but not the right to vote. At about the same time, **Unionists** in Arkansas formed a new government. It, too, ended slavery.

President and Congress Clash

Some members of Lincoln's Republican party did not like his 10-percent policy.

THE AFTERMATH OF THE CIVIL WAR

They thought that 50 percent of all white males in the state should take the oath before a new government could be formed. They also wanted to make sure that the new governments excluded Confederates. Only people who could take an "ironclad oath" that they had never supported the Confederacy would be allowed in the new government. Finally, those Republicans wanted to permanently end slavery; the Emancipation Proclamation had only ended slavery as a policy of war.

On July 4, 1864, Congress passed the Wade-Davis Bill, which put these changes into effect. Lincoln disliked the bill; he wanted to keep Recon-

struction more flexible. Also, the bill would have voided the new governments of Louisiana and Arkansas, and he did not want to move backward. Finally, he did not think Congress had the power to end slavery. As a result, he **vetoed** the bill, which meant that it never became law.

Reconstruction at Lincoln's Death

By early 1865, Lincoln and Republican leaders in Congress had moved closer together. Lincoln agreed to give the vote to African Americans who had served as soldiers—partly meeting another goal of the congressional leaders. They, in turn, agreed that the new version of the Wade-Davis Bill would accept the governments of Louisiana and Arkansas and a newly formed one in Tennessee. Once again, however, Democrats in Congress managed to block passage of the bill.

Meanwhile, Lincoln had continued to urge a moderate course toward white Southerners. When he took the oath of office as president a second time on March 4, 1865, he expressed his wish to build a "just and a lasting peace" in which North and South would reunite "with malice toward none" and "with charity for all." Little more than a month later, however, John Wilkes Booth, an actor and fervent supporter of the Confederacy,

EMANCIPATION MADE COMPLETE

*Lincoln thought the only legal route to ending slavery permanently was to pass an **amendment** to the U.S. Constitution. The U.S. Senate had passed such an amendment back in April of 1864, but Democrats had enough power in the House of Representatives to defeat it there. Lincoln urged Congress to act again, and early in 1865, the Thirteenth Amendment ending slavery finally was passed. By the end of the year, it had been **ratified** by enough states to make it part of the Constitution. Finally, slavery was dead.*

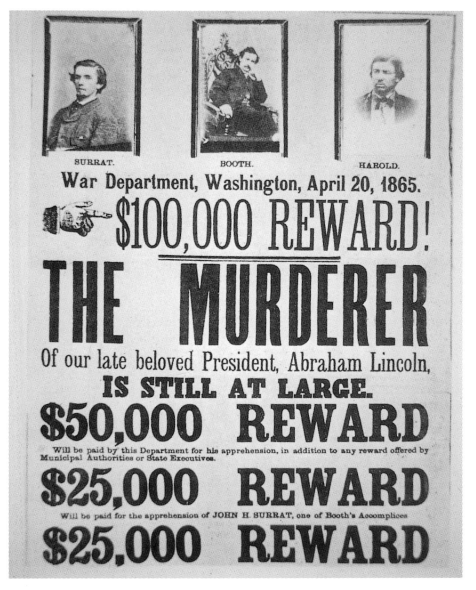

SURRAT.   BOOTH.   HAROLD.

War Department, Washington, April 20, 1865.

☛ $100,000 REWARD!

THE MURDERER

Of our late beloved President, Abraham Lincoln,

IS STILL AT LARGE.

$50,000 REWARD

Will be paid by this Department for his apprehension, in addition to any reward offered by Municipal Authorities or State Executives.

$25,000 REWARD

Will be paid for the apprehension of JOHN H. SURRAT, one of Booth's Accomplices

$25,000 REWARD

John Wilkes Booth, Lincoln's assassin, was trapped in a Virginia barn and killed less than a week after this poster was issued. David Herold (the poster misspells his name), John Surrat's mother, and two others were found guilty of helping Booth and hanged. While John Surrat escaped to Canada, he was later captured and tried for joining in the assassination plot. The jury could not agree on a guilty verdict, and he remained free.

assassinated Lincoln in Ford's Theatre in Washington, D.C. Vice President Andrew Johnson became president. He would have to work with Congress to answer the questions about the Reconstruction of the South.

CHAPTER THREE

African Americans in the South

*"I felt like
a bird out of a cage. Amen.
Amen. Amen. I could hardly ask to
feel any better than I did that day."*

Former slave Houston Holloway, remembering
the day he learned of emancipation

Experiencing Freedom

While leaders in Washington debated Reconstruction, African Americans in the South were living a revolution. Now they could go where they wanted, marry whom they wished, choose their own employer, make daily decisions of their own, testify in court, and live as they wanted.

Many blacks took advantage of their freedom to move; many traveled from plantations to cities, hoping to find jobs and to gain protection from Union soldiers stationed there. Others walked to other counties or states, hoping to rejoin spouses, parents, or children who had been sold away from them years before.

Building New Institutions

Many African Americans quickly took steps to shape their futures. They joined together to build new institutions to give strength to their communities. Churches were often the first institutions they formed. These churches met more than just religious needs; they were social meeting places. Church leaders became important figures in black communities, influencing politics.

Many of the churches included schools, which were new institutions for former slaves. Visitors to the South commented often on how hungry African Americans were to learn how to read and write. A white from Tennessee noted

Churches played vital roles in the lives of newly freed African Americans.

that blacks were so eager to learn that "they will starve themselves . . . to send their children to school." Many of the teachers were blacks who had been free before the war.

The Freedmen's Bureau

Congress saw that the government needed to do something to help the former slaves, or freedmen, so in March 1865, it passed a law creating the Freedmen's Bureau. This organization's task was to provide food and clothing to those in the South who needed it—including whites. It was also supposed to help African Americans move smoothly into a life of freedom.

The Freedmen's Bureau built more than four thousand schools and helped establish a few black colleges, some of which still stand. Bureau workers tried to protect blacks from the violence sometimes directed against them. They also set up temporary courts and tried to help landowners and free blacks agree on labor contracts.

The Bureau had too much to do and too few people to do it, however.

Before the Civil War, state laws in the South made it illegal to teach enslaved African Americans to read and write. After the war, thousands of blacks—adults as well as children—poured into schools like this one to grab their newfound chance to learn.

Major General O. O. Howard, head of the Freedmen's Bureau, never had more than about nine hundred workers spread across the entire South. It could not meet all the needs of the African Americans or settle all the conflicts between Southern blacks and whites.

Promises Made but Not Kept

Late in the war, Union general William Sherman boldly moved to help freed African Americans. Thousands of blacks had attached themselves to his army. In January 1865, he issued an order promising each family 40 acres (16 hectares) of land. The order said they could hold the land temporarily until Congress gave them formal ownership. By the summer of 1865, nearly forty thousand blacks were settled on land in South Carolina. Howard backed the effort and in July told his officers across the South to give land to freedmen.

However, President Andrew Johnson feared that if blacks had their own land, they would become too independent. Alhough he had opposed the South leaving the Union, he still wanted to make sure that whites ran the economy and governments of the South. Unwilling to accept Sherman's action, President Johnson ordered Howard to return the land to its former owners.

African Americans reacted bitterly. One protested that he was being asked to "forgive . . . the man who tied me to a tree and gave me 39 lashes." Nevertheless, Johnson's order prevailed.

The government also let blacks down in another way. The Freedmen's Bureau began pressuring freedmen to sign labor contracts with white planters, contracts that guaranteed blacks would be paid for their work—although at low wages. Some also made clear that planters could no longer physically punish black workers, as they had done to slaves. Still, the contracts severely limited the rights of black workers. Over time, the Bureau stopped playing any role in settling disputes over work issues between whites and freedmen. The freedmen were left on their own, with no one to protect them.

Harper's Weekly, a Northern illustrated journal, saw the Freedmen's Bureau as responsible for maintaining peace between Southern whites and newly freed blacks.

CHAPTER FOUR

President and Congress Fight

*"What
scares [Northerners] is the
idea that the rebels are all to be let
back . . . and made a power in the
government again, just as though there
had been no rebellion."*

Charles A. Dana, Chicago newspaper
editor, 1865

Johnson's Plan

When Andrew Johnson became president, Congress was not in session, giving Johnson several months to act without congressional interference. He moved quickly. In late May 1865, Johnson issued two presidential proclamations outlining his plan for Reconstruction.

In the first, Johnson offered amnesty to most who had fought for the South if they swore loyalty to the Constitution. There were exceptions, such as Confederate government officials, but even these people could appeal to him for a pardon. Over time, Johnson granted thousands of these appeals.

The other proclamation covered how new state governments would be formed. He would name temporary governors, who would call a convention of their state's people. Those who attended would then set the rules for who could hold office in the new state governments.

New Governments

The temporary governors that Johnson appointed quickly called conventions. In most states, these meetings repealed the vote for secession, abolished slavery, and set dates for statewide elections. The elections were held, and new legislatures met. Many of these bodies approved the Thirteenth Amendment, which ended slavery. By the end of 1865, all the states had new governments. They sent new senators and representatives to Washington, D.C., to sit in the U.S. Congress.

In the states of the Upper South, such as Virginia, North Carolina, Tennessee, and Arkansas, most of the new officeholders had been Unionists before the war. In states farther south, however, many were former Confederates. Even Alexander Stephens, the vice president of the Confederacy, was elected senator of Georgia, which annoyed some Northerners.

Northerners were even more angered by laws the new state legislatures passed. The states' Black Codes sharply limited the rights of African Americans. Under these laws, blacks who wanted to do any work other than farm labor had to pay a fee. Those who did not have jobs could be arrested. Orphans could be seized by landowners and forced to work for them.

Many in the North were also angered by reports of violent attacks on blacks in the South. Growing numbers of Republicans came to believe that freedmen should be given the right to vote so they could protect their rights.

ANDREW JOHNSON

Born in North Carolina in 1808, Andrew Johnson was plunged into poverty at age three when his father died. At seventeen, he moved to Tennessee and opened a tailor's shop, teaching himself to read and write.

Johnson became active politically at age twenty-one, representing poor people who had little voice in government. He served in Tennessee's state legislature, in the U.S. House and Senate, and as Tennessee's governor. Though a Democrat, he was loyal to the Union. When the South seceded, he was the only Southern senator to stay in the Senate. He despised the wealthy planters who dominated Southern politics.

In 1865, Johnson became president when Lincoln was killed. After finishing out the term, he returned to Tennessee. Johnson lost a Senate race in 1869 and a House election in 1872. In 1875, he was elected to the Senate but died that same year.

A group of freed blacks poses in one of the South's shattered cities. Freedmen moved to Southern cities in large numbers, hoping to escape farm work and find well-paying jobs. The South's poor economy and its large supply of workers held down wages, forcing most urban blacks to live in poverty.

The Republicans Respond

In December 1865, Congress began meeting again. Republican leaders moved to gain control over Reconstruction, refusing to recognize the representatives from the new state governments. Outraged by the Black Codes, they pushed through a civil rights bill. This law, passed in April 1866, declared that blacks were citizens and that all citizens had equal rights. Congress also passed the Fourteenth Amendment, which placed equality firmly in the Constitution and gave African Americans the right to vote.

President Johnson disapproved of these steps. He vetoed the Civil Rights Act, but the bill became law anyway when Congress overrode his veto. He also sent a message to the states urging them not to approve the Fourteenth Amendment. Soon after, the legislatures of every former Confederate state except Tennessee voted against it. These votes killed the amendment—and angered Republicans in Congress even more.

Johnson against the Congress

To make his policies into law, Johnson needed more support in Congress. He began campaigning against Republicans in the upcoming congressional elections and backed Democrats, even former Confederates. Voters turned out in huge numbers to elect Republican candidates, however. The party won a 42–11 majority in the Senate and a 143–49 majority in the House. The congressional leaders rejoiced, knowing that they could control Reconstruction since they had more than enough votes to override any presidential vetoes.

The new Congress quickly passed the Reconstruction Act of 1867, which placed the Southern states under military governors. In addition, every Southern state had to ratify the Fourteenth Amendment before Congress would recognize its government.

Impeachment

Congress also passed the Tenure of Office Act, which said that a president could not remove from office an official whom the Senate had approved. The law had a clear aim—to prevent Johnson from firing any Cabinet members.

Secretary of War Edwin Stanton, an ally of the Republicans in Congress, had clashed with President Johnson over Reconstruction policy. Finally, early in 1868, Johnson tried to fire Stanton, violating the Tenure of Office Act. The next day, Thaddeus Stevens, the U.S. representative from Pennsylvania, offered the House a resolution for the **impeachment** of the president. The

This ticket allowed a guest to sit in the gallery—the upper portion of the Senate chamber—and watch the arguments for and against impeaching Andrew Johnson. The trial marked the first time in U.S. history that a president was impeached.

In the ten days after the failure to win the first vote on impeachment, Republicans put intense pressure on senators. On May 26, Edmund Ross of Kansas, in a voice barely heard in a still chamber, said "not guilty," stopping the Senate from removing President Andrew Johnson from office by just one vote.

House voted in favor of several articles of impeachment. The president was to be tried by the Senate—for the first time in history.

The trial began a few weeks later. A dying Thaddeus Stevens spoke harshly against the president—and anyone who dared to vote in his favor. On March 16, a key article of impeachment came to a vote.

> "[Stanton,] who had been watching the call with breathless interest, turned ghastly pale; as he rose to leave the chamber he staggered so that Gen. Logan took his arm and helped him away. . . . Poor old lame Thaddeus Stevens rose up and shambled out, neither asking [for] or receiving support; he limped out on his crutch, his face plainly showing the venomous but now futile hatred of Johnson and of the South which scarred his soul."
>
> Minor Meriwether, a witness to the impeachment vote, 1868

The Republicans were one vote short of finding Johnson guilty. Ten days later, the Senate voted down the other articles of impeachment.

As a result, Andrew Johnson remained in office for the rest of his term. In the fall of 1868, Union general and war hero Ulysses S. Grant was elected president as a Republican. He took office the following March.

CHAPTER FIVE

Changes in the South

~

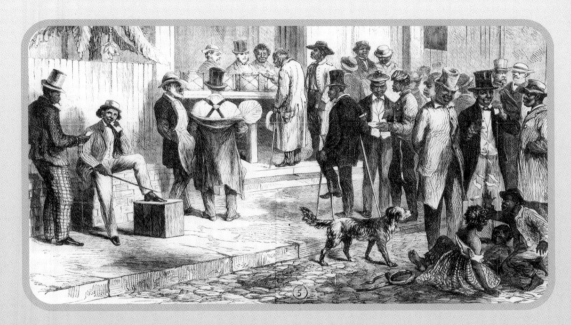

This 1867 illustration shows African Americans in New Orleans exercising their newly won right to vote.

New Governments Form Again

Under the new Reconstruction laws, only Tennessee was allowed back in the Union. The other Southern states had to form new governments again.

At first, white Southerners delayed acting. Many did not wish to give equal rights—especially voting rights—to blacks. Congress responded with a new law that allowed the military commanders in the South to call the conventions and to register voters. Republicans dominated those conventions.

Republicans in the South came from three groups. The largest group was freedmen, who saw the Republican Party as their chance to gain vital rights. Though they were the most numerous Republicans, blacks were not a majority of convention delegates. The next largest group was Southern Unionists, nicknamed the "scalawags" by other Southern whites. The third group was called the "carpetbaggers." These were Northerners who had moved to the South to help the freedmen or to look for business opportunities. The Southern whites who opposed Reconstruction viewed scalawags as traitors and carpetbaggers as invaders.

One issue facing the state conventions was whether to take away the voting rights of former Confederates. Scalawags tended to back this policy. However,

"I have no desire to take away the rights of the white man. All I want is equal rights in the court house and equal rights when I go to vote."

Thomas Lee, a freedman and a member of the Alabama convention, 1867

many African Americans felt that reducing anyone's right to vote was not a good idea. In the end, only the states of Louisiana, Arkansas, and Alabama blocked large numbers of former Confederates from voting.

"Black Reconstruction"

The period following the conventions is often called "Black Reconstruction" because African Americans played important roles in the new governments. Sixteen served in the U.S. Congress,

The first African Americans to serve in Congress posed for this picture. Mississippi's Hiram Revels, the only senator of the group, is seated farthest left. The other seated figures are (from front left) Alabama's Benjamin Turner, Florida's Josiah Walls, and Joseph Raney and Robert Elliott of South Carolina. Behind them stand (left) South Carolina's Robert DeLarge and Georgia's Jefferson Long.

including two—Hiram Revels and Blanche K. Bruce—in the Senate. About two thousand African Americans won state offices across the South. Still, the name "Black Reconstruction" is somewhat misleading. Blacks formed a majority in the state legislatures only in South Carolina, and few reached high statewide office.

White Southerners blasted the new governments as corrupt and incompetent. While there was some corruption, the same had been true before the war; these white Southerners were simply criticizing the new state governments to lessen support for them. However, the new governments passed many laws to better the South. They set up public school systems and, in two states, public colleges. They also tried to promote economic growth and the need to rebuild the shattered South. One thing that hurt the new governments in the South was that these ambitious plans required money, which meant that the governments had to raise taxes.

White Resistance

The majority of white Southerners worked to block the new laws. They tried to win support by railing against high taxes; they also strongly appealed to white racism.

ROBERT ELLIOTT

Robert Elliott was born in 1842, but much of his early life is unclear. By 1867, though, he and his wife lived in Charleston, South Carolina.

There, Elliott became an editor of a new, black-owned newspaper and entered politics. In 1868, he was a member of the convention formed to write a new state constitution. After one term in the state legislature, he was elected to the U.S. House, where he served two terms. In his first speech, he rose to protest a bill that would extend full civil rights to ex-Confederates.

Returning to South Carolina, Elliott became speaker of the state house of representatives. When white Southern Democrats regained control of the state government, though, he lost his office. He moved to New Orleans in 1881 to practice law. He died three years later.

Some Southern whites used terror to push their opposition to Reconstruction. A secret organization called the Ku Klux Klan had formed shortly after the war. During the late 1860s, it spread and became much more active. Wearing white hoods, Klan members terrorized blacks as well as white Republicans. They beat—and sometimes killed—blacks for voting for Republicans. They attacked elected officials and even people who were teaching freedmen to read and write. Some estimates say that as many as 20,000 people were killed by the Klan in just a few years.

The governors of Alabama, Texas, and Tennessee moved strongly against Klan violence in

Members of the Ku Klux Klan wore hooded disguises and struck at night. Congress passed tough laws that put down the Klan, but other racist groups rose in its place.

"Of the slain, there were enough to furnish forth a battlefield, and all from those three classes, the negro, the scalawag, and the carpet-bagger,—all killed with deliberation, overwhelmed by numbers, roused from slumber at the murky midnight, in the hall of public assembly, upon the river-brink, on the lonely woods-road."

Albion Tourgée on the actions of the Klan, 1879

their states. In 1870 and 1871, the U.S. Congress passed two Ku Klux Klan Acts that made it a federal crime to conspire to deny citizens their rights. Hundreds of people were arrested across the South. By 1872, the power of the Klan had been broken.

Economic Problems

Forceful action taken against the Klan spared blacks further widespread violence. Still, the freedmen's position in the 1870s was not strong, mainly as a result of the economic situation. The federal government had not broken up the Southern plantations. Unless African Americans were given some land so they could earn their living, they were doomed to an inferior

This colorful 1870 print celebrates the many newfound freedoms of Southern blacks. Although African Americans were now free, they faced uncertain futures.

position in society. Most lawmakers, however, were unwilling to take the step and give them land.

Because a few whites controlled most of the land, they had the power to force most blacks into a new system that was not much better than slavery—sharecropping. In sharecropping, a plantation owner agreed to let a family farm a plot of land. In return, the family gave part of its crop to the owner. This system appealed to many blacks because it gave them a chance to work the land as families,

> *"In this 'land of the free' we are burned, tortured, and denied a fair trial, murdered for any imaginary wrong conceived in the brain of the negro-hating white man. There is no [help] for us from a government which promised to protect all under its flag."*
>
> Susie King Taylor in 1902; she escaped slavery in 1862

Some Southern blacks found life in the South impossible after the war. This family moved to Nebraska, where it used the Homestead Act to obtain cheap land to farm.

not as parts of a plantation gang. Over time, though, families had to borrow money for supplies and tools. When cotton prices fell, they could not repay the loans. As the years passed, they fell further into debt but were still tied to farming for the owner of the plantation.

"I ask you [of the North] to take the hand held out to you by your Southern brethren . . . and say . . . 'The war is ended, let us again be fellow countrymen, and forget that we have been enemies.'"

Horace Greeley, newspaper
editor, 1872

Changing Attitudes in the North

Northern outrage had helped spur the government to act against the Klan in 1870 and 1871. By 1873, though, many

Northerners were less interested in Reconstruction; they had tired of the issue. In addition, hatred of Southerners had lessened as time passed.

Also, many Northerners were distracted by growing concern over the corruption in Washington, D.C. In 1872, newspapers were full of stories of members of the government gaining wealth by selling their votes.

In addition, an economic disaster hit in late 1873. Thousands lost their jobs in an economic slump that lasted five years. Facing an uncertain future, many Northerners grew less concerned with the South's problems.

Hard economic times and government scandals caused problems for Republicans in the 1874 congressional elections; Democrats won a solid majority in the U.S. House. At the same time, the power of the white conservatives in the South was growing. Appeals to their prejudice against African Americans had persuaded many scalawags (Southern Unionists) to leave the Republican Party. From 1870 to 1876, most of the South fell into the hands of these antiblack forces. By 1876, only three Southern states remained in the hands of the Republicans.

President Ulysses S. Grant's vice president, Schuyler Colfax, shown here, was one of several government members who took payments from powerful business leaders. This and other scandals weakened the Republican Party and shifted national attention away from the South.

The End of Reconstruction

The presidential election of 1876 between Republican Rutherford B. Hayes and Democrat Samuel J. Tilden

"Negroes must insist continually . . . that voting is necessary to proper manhood, that color discrimination is barbarism, and that black boys need education as well as white boys."

W. E. B. Du Bois, *The Souls of Black Folk*, 1903

was the closest presidential race since 1824. Tilden won the popular vote but was one vote short of a majority in the electoral college, which actually decides who becomes president. There were also disputes over twenty of the electoral votes, most of them from the South.

Politicians struggled to settle the contest but finally worked out a deal. Hayes agreed that if he won the disputed votes and became president, he would pull out the federal troops that were propping up the three remaining Republican governments in the South. Removing the soldiers would allow the Southern whites to regain control of those states. Once Hayes took office, he withdrew the troops. White governments took power in Florida, Louisiana, and South Carolina. In effect, Reconstruction was now over.

Wade Hampton, a rich planter before the war and a Confederate general during it, became South Carolina's new governor after the 1876 election put whites back in control of Southern state governments.

"Jim Crow" Takes Control

White-run governments in the South began passing "Jim Crow" laws that limited the civil rights of African Americans. These laws put in place segregation, which was designed to keep blacks and whites apart. African Americans had to attend separate schools, ride their own railroad cars, and go to their own restaurants. In most cases, those separate African-American facilities were inferior to the ones provided to whites.

In 1875, Congress passed a far-reaching Civil Rights Act. The law said that all people, black and white, should enjoy equal access to restaurants, public transportation, and other facilities. The law could have been used to break segregation, but it was never enforced. Finally, a Supreme Court decision upheld the "Jim Crow" laws and doomed blacks to second-class citizenship. In 1896, the Court ruled in *Plessy* v. *Ferguson* that "separate but equal" facilities for blacks and whites were acceptable under the Constitution. As a result, segregation became firmly entrenched in the South. Eventually, southern states passed laws that curtailed blacks' right to vote. Many African Americans protested, but the federal government did nothing to help them.

This cartoon shows Columbia—a symbol of the United States—handing the Civil Rights Act to an African American eager for equality. After the end of Reconstruction, however, blacks suffered decades of unequal treatment that the government did nothing to stop.

Impact of the War on the North

John Weir's painting *Forging the Shaft* symbolizes the heavy industries—iron, coal, steel, railroad—that grew after the Civil War.

Economic Impact

The early postwar period saw a tremendous economic boom in the North. Much of that boom came from industry. In 1873, the nation's factories produced 75 percent more goods than they had in 1865. Most of that growth came in the North, where cities became industrial centers.

Agriculture also grew. New machines—produced in northern factories—helped farmers plant and harvest their crops in less time than before. In addition, new areas were settled. From 1860 to 1880, the population of Minnesota,

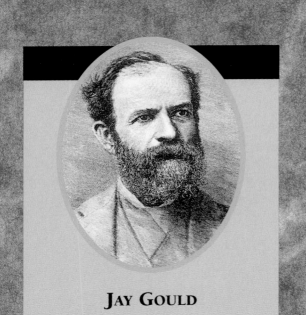

JAY GOULD

Born in New York City in 1836, Jay Gould worked at several different jobs before the Civil War. Then he became involved in buying and selling railroad stock, which laid the foundation of his fortune. By 1867, he and partners had gained control of the Erie Railroad, an important New York line. They used several illegal tactics—including bribing state lawmakers—to maintain that control. In 1869, he and his associates caused a financial panic by causing the value of gold to collapse. The outcry against him forced Gould to sell the Erie line.

Still, he had a fortune of more than $25 million and a desire for more. Gould gobbled up railroad lines until he owned about 15 percent of all track in the country. By the time he died in 1892, he had amassed a fortune of nearly $80 million.

the Dakotas, Kansas, and Nebraska mushroomed from 300,000 to more than 2 million. Many settlers took advantage of the Homestead Act of 1862, which made western land available at very low prices. The coming of these settlers pushed out the Native Americans who had lived on the Great Plains. Though many resisted, the Indians were forced to move onto reservations.

Carrying those settlers to the Plains were the railroads. After the war, railroads spread across the North and the West. From 1865 to 1873, 35,000 miles (56,000 kilometers) of track were put down—more railroad track than had existed in the entire country before the war. At the same time, large railroad companies gobbled up smaller ones. The owners of those lines, like Jay Gould, became fabulously wealthy. Other giant corporations grew as well. Iron and steel became big businesses as did lumber and mining. The depression that hit in 1873 hurt many of these wealthy industrialists—and it clobbered workers.

Women's lives also changed somewhat. Millions of women labored hard on family farms, as they had before the war, but more began working in industry. By 1900, about one in four wage-earning workers were women, far more than before the war.

During the 1850s, Congress had authorized work to find the best route for the railroad to take from the Great Plains to the West Coast. Lawmakers from the North and South, however, fought over which route to choose. When the Southern states left the Union, the North was free to choose the path it favored. In 1862, Congress passed the Pacific Railroad Act, which favored the northern route.

Soon, the Central Pacific Railroad began building track from San Francisco eastward. Thousands of Chinese laborers did the back-breaking work of moving the line through California's mountains and across the Nevada desert. The Union Pacific, beginning in Omaha, built

Workers constructed many bridges like this one to carry the railroad from the Pacific Ocean through the high mountains of eastern California.

track toward the west, with Irish laborers and former soldiers laying the track. The two lines met near Promontory Point, Utah, in 1869. As workers cheered, railroad officials and politicians celebrated completing the railroad by driving a golden spike into the line.

However, working women generally were paid less than working men.

Political Impact

Initially, Republicans dominated postwar politics in the North. One way they achieved success was to identify themselves with having saved the Union. The Democrats, they charged, had been willing to give up. This approach to campaigning came to be called "waving the bloody shirt."

They were aided in this by the formation of the Grand Army of the Republic, a veterans' group organized in 1866 that was closely linked to the Republican Party. The Grand Army pushed for certain issues, especially pensions for disabled veterans.

Millions of immigrants came to the United States in the late 1800s, helping to power the country's economic growth. This scene shows families eating a meal at the Ellis Island entry station in New York City's harbor.

Still, the Democratic Party had its own power. The nation's cities were growing as people flocked to work in urban factories. Many of these new workers came from the increasing number of immigrants from Europe, who often settled in the growing Northern cities. With little interest in blacks' rights, workers and immigrants tended to join the Democratic Party. Indeed, many feared that African Americans would take their jobs from them. The support of these voters helped the Democrats build powerful political organizations in the cities. They also helped the party gain at the national level. By 1876, Democrats had regained control of the House and almost won the presidency. For about the next twenty years, the Democrats and Republicans were roughly equal in power.

CHAPTER SEVEN

Perspectives on the War

Paying Tribute

After the war, many on both sides wished to pay tribute to the men who had fought and died. In 1866, the people of Columbus, Mississippi, and Waterloo, New York, separately set aside a day to remember the war dead from their communities. Two years later, the head of the Grand Army of the Republic, John Logan, named May 30 as a day for "decorating the graves of comrades who died in defense of their country." The holiday, called "Decoration Day," spread across the country. Today, it is the national holiday known as Memorial Day.

Local communities also built monuments and statues to honor the soldiers and sailors from their town. Veterans' groups formed in both North and South to aid disabled veterans and their families and campaign to save the war's battlefields. The Daughters of the Confederacy, limited to women whose fathers were veterans, did much to

This postcard from around the end of the 1800s honored both sides in the war and was used to celebrate Memorial Day.

Reenactors, such as these people dressed as Union troops, carefully research their uniforms and supplies to ensure they accurately reflect those used during the Civil War.

honor Southern soldiers. At its peak, this group contained more than 40,000 members.

Interest in life during the Civil War continues. Thousands of Civil War enthusiasts have formed reenactment groups, steeping themselves in the history of the war. Dressed in replica uniforms and carrying period weapons, they stage mock fights on the anniversaries of significant battles.

The Civil War has also entered the Internet age. Internet discussion groups give historians—professional and amateur—a chance to share their knowledge and argue their unique perspectives on the war.

"Old soldiers tended to measure each other as preservers of an older, more wholesome society, uncorrupted . . . and rooted in individual honor. They came to see their war experience as a special, shared possession, and the battlefields where they reassembled 20 or 30 years after the fact as their own sites of healing."

Historian David Blight, 2002

Civil War Library

More than 50,000 books have been written about the Civil War, with hundreds more published every year. It is, one prominent historian says, "the most written-about event in American history."

Soon after the war, participants offered accounts of their own experiences. Some were generals trying to

Soon after the war, the Daughters of the Confederacy bought former battlefields in the South. They wanted to dedicate the sites to the Confederate dead as part of the effort to remember the "Lost Cause." Later, the government took control of many battlefields. Today, more than two dozen national battlefield parks attract thousands of visitors every year.

For many years, tours and museum exhibits at these parks focused on telling the stories of the battles. Their aim was to show soldiers on both sides as heroes.

The Gettysburg National Cemetery was one of the first Civil War battlefields to become a national park.

This approach ignored the issue of slavery. Recently, however, the National Park Service has begun giving a broader picture of the war, including information about slavery.

justify their own decisions. Ordinary soldiers and low-ranking officers also wrote many of these personal accounts, giving valuable glimpses into the lives and thinking of the people who did the actual fighting.

Historians have taken many approaches to studying the war. Some monumental works cover it in detail. Others have focused on specific aspects of the war, such as medicine, prisons, or diplomacy. Thousands of books have been written about Abraham Lincoln alone. In recent years, many books have tried to tell how the war affected ordinary men and women.

One of the first of the many fictional accounts of the war was Union veteran John William De Forest's *Miss Ravenel's Conversion from Secession to Loyalty*. The novel used the marriage of a Northern officer and a Southern woman to present a vision of reconciliation between the two sides.

Other novels focus on the lives of split families or recount individual battles. Perhaps the most famous

In the early 1880s, Union general and former president Ulysses S. Grant was poor because of bad investments and dying of throat cancer. Wrapped in warm clothing, he spent the last months of his life writing his memoirs on the porch of his home.

Civil War novel is *Gone with the Wind*. Margaret Mitchell's sprawling book carries the reader through the Civil War and Reconstruction using the perspective of a spirited Southern daughter of a plantation owner. It presents a romantic, positive image of the South and the suffering of its whites during and after the war. Slavery is not criticized. The book did much to shape the way many Americans saw the Civil War. Later books, both historical and fictional, have tried to counter this romantic view of the South.

Pictures of the War

People have also used pictures to tell the story of the Civil War. Until the early 1900s, these efforts were limited to still photographs and prints. In 1915, however, film director D. W. Griffith made *The Birth of a Nation*, a silent movie that told the story of the war on an epic scale. While Griffith's work was the first full-length movie, its appeal today is clouded by its racist portrayal of African Americans.

A more recent movie, *Glory*, released in 1989, has offered a different perspective, telling the story of

Gone with the Wind became the best-selling novel of all time. The book was also made into a highly successful movie, advertised in this poster.

MARGARET MITCHELL

Born in 1900 in Georgia, Margaret Mitchell learned about the Civil War from family stories, which reflected the views of Southern whites. In the late 1920s, she began working on Gone With the Wind. Published in 1936, the book was a huge— and immediate—success, selling a million copies in the first year alone. Mitchell, overwhelmed by her success, never wrote another book. She died in 1949.

the black soldiers who fought in the Fifty-fourth Massachusetts infantry regiment. In doing so, it convincingly presents what the Civil War—and freedom—meant to African Americans.

Perhaps the most notable visual presentation on the war, though, is Ken Burns's *The Civil War,* first shown in 1990. This thirteen-hour television documentary uses contemporary images, actors speaking the words of participants, and interviews with historians and scholars to portray the war from many points of view.

CHAPTER EIGHT

The Lasting Impact

~

This 1914 photograph of two veterans of the Civil War, one Northern and one Southern, shaking hands reflects the view of the late 1800s that the nation had overcome the bitterness of the war years and should honor the troops of both sides.

"One Nation, Indivisible"

The Civil War brought about many far-reaching changes in the United States. Louisiana planter Richard Taylor commented in December 1865 that "society has been completely changed by the war." Some of those differences still affect Americans today. One important effect of the Civil War was in how Americans viewed their country. Before the Civil War, people tended to see themselves as citizens of a state first and of the country second. Afterward, people tended to view themselves as citizens of a nation. Before the war, people typically said "the United States are," emphasizing the individual states. After the war, they said "the United States is," stressing the unified nation.

This change was not complete. Sectional differences remained for many decades. Some Southerners mistrusted Northerners. Many Northerners felt superior to the Southerners. It took until the 1950s and later for many of these differences to lessen.

The national government also became stronger in the Civil War than it had ever been. This was in part because the demands of the war required a stronger federal role.

"Free at Last"

The most notable change, however, was the end of slavery for about 4 million African Americans as a result of the Thirteenth Amendment. Blacks celebrated the realization of a long-cherished dream. "Old men and women weep and shout for joy," journalist T. Morris Chester wrote.

The end of slavery brought not only dramatic personal changes; it was also a major social change. The

REPARATIONS?

Although African-American slaves were freed by the Civil War, they still suffered discrimination. Some people say that the government should pay **reparations** *to their descendants. Others agree that slavery was wrong but say that people alive today had nothing to do with it; they should not be forced to pay for an injustice they were not responsible for. The debate continues.*

economic and social structures of the South were built on slavery. Clearly, Southerners—black and white—would have to build new relationships as a result of emancipation.

A Promise Unfulfilled

While blacks gained freedom, they were denied equality. The end of Reconstruction left whites dominating the South once again. "Jim Crow" laws forced African Americans into rundown schools and dead-end jobs across the South. The North also had laws and customs that blocked equal access to many aspects of life for African Americans.

Many African Americans and others worked to end this discrimination, but the struggle has taken decades. In the 1950s and 1960s, the

This 1963 demonstration in Birmingham, Alabama, was part of the civil rights movement that swept the country in the 1950s and 1960s. Here, three demonstrators hold hands as riot police use powerful hoses to try to knock them down with water.

civil rights movement gained ground. One reason was the inspirational leadership of Martin Luther King Jr., and others. Another was recognition by many whites that the unequal treatment was unfair.

This movement brought about many positive changes for black Americans. By the end of the 1900s, African Americans were in a better position in many ways. Relations between the races were generally more comfortable and friendly than in the past.

Still, problems persisted. Blacks were more likely than whites to be

Attorney Thurgood Marshall (center) and two colleagues celebrate the Supreme Court's 1954 decision that said that segregated schools were illegal. These lawyers argued the case against segregated schools before the Court. About a decade later, Marshall became the first African American to serve as a justice of the Supreme Court.

poor and to be unemployed. Schools had become increasingly segregated, and those with mostly black students tended to be of poorer quality. Some African Americans had been victims of vicious hate crimes. Clearly, work remained to be done before the dream of complete equality between the races could be realized. The Civil War, which finally brought about the end of slavery, was the first step on the long road to that goal.

MARTIN LUTHER KING. JR.

Born in Atlanta, Georgia, in 1929, Martin Luther King entered college at age fifteen. When he graduated, he decided to become a minister.

*King became pastor at a black church in Montgomery, Alabama. Soon after, the city's African Americans began to **boycott** against the city's segregated buses, with King as a strong and eloquent leader. He became the major figure in the civil rights movement, always cautioning his followers to use **nonviolent resistance**. In a massive march on Washington in 1963, King delivered his most famous speech, expressing his dream that one day black and white Americans could live in peace and equality.*

In 1964, King was awarded the Nobel Prize for Peace. In 1968, he was shot and killed. Americans across the country mourned his death. In 1986, Congress voted to name a national holiday in his honor.

1863 *Jan. 1:* President Abraham Lincoln issues Emancipation Proclamation.
Dec. 8: Lincoln offers 10-percent plan, which made it relatively easy for Southern states to return to the Union.

1864 *July 4:* Congress approves Wade-Davis Bill, setting tougher rules for Southern states to reenter the Union.
July 8: Lincoln vetoes Wade-Davis Bill.

1865 *Jan. 16:* Major General William Sherman issues order promising land to former slaves for farming.
Jan. 31: Congress passes Thirteenth Amendment, ending slavery.
Mar. 3: Congress passes law creating Freedmen's Bureau to help African Americans switch to life in freedom.
Apr. 15: Lincoln assassinated; Vice President Andrew Johnson becomes president.
May 29: Johnson issues two Reconstruction proclamations that set easy terms for reformed Southern governments.
Dec. 6: Thirteenth Amendment ratified.

1866 *Apr. 9:* Congress passes Civil Rights Act by overriding Johnson's veto.
June 16: Congress approves the Fourteenth Amendment, which makes African Americans citizens.
July 24: Tennessee accepted into Union.
Nov.: Republicans win overwhelming majority in Congress.

1867 *Mar. 2:* Congress passes Reconstruction Act over Johnson's veto.
Mar. 2: Congress passes Tenure of Office Act, which prevents a president from removing from office any official who has been approved by Congress.

1868 *Feb. 24:* House approves resolution impeaching Johnson.
May 16: Johnson found not guilty of key impeachment article; final vote of acquittal comes ten days later.
June 22: Arkansas accepted into Union.
June 25: Alabama, Florida, Louisiana, North Carolina, and South Carolina formally accepted back into the Union.
Nov. 3: Former Union general Ulysses S. Grant elected president.

1869 *May 10:* Transcontinental railroad completed.

1870 *Jan. 26:* Virginia accepted into Union.
Feb. 23: Mississippi accepted into Union.
Feb. 25: Hiram Revels of Mississippi becomes first African-American senator.
Mar. 30: Texas accepted into Union.
May 31: Congress passes first Ku Klux Klan Act, trying to stop violence against Southern blacks.
July 15: Georgia accepted into Union.

1871 *Apr. 20:* Congress passes second Ku Klux Klan Act.

1873 *Sep. 18:* Failure of financial firm launches the Panic of 1873, a depression that lasts five years; economic worries in the North turn attention away from Reconstruction.

1875 *Mar. 1:* U.S. Congress passes Civil Rights Act, but it is never enforced.

1876 *Nov. 7:* Rutherford B. Hayes and Samuel J. Tilden finish the presidential election in a virtual tie.

1877 *Mar. 2:* Senate announces that Hayes will be president; he has gained office by promising to take federal troops out of the South.

Apr. 24: Last federal troops withdrawn from South; last state government falls into hands of Southern whites.

1896 **May 18:** Supreme Court rules in *Plessy* v. *Ferguson* that "separate but equal" facilities for blacks and whites are constitutional; decision allows "Jim Crow" laws, which discriminate against blacks, to stand.

1954 **May 17:** Supreme Court rules in *Brown* v. *Board of Education* that in public education "separate but equal" facilities are not constitutional.

Glossary

amendment: a formal change to a constitution.

amnesty: a pardon granted to a group of people guilty of political crimes.

amputation: an operation in which a surgeon cuts off a severely damaged limb.

bond: a loan in which an investor pays the government a certain amount of money and receives the promise that it will repay that money, plus interest, at a later date.

Border States: the states on the northern edge of the southern states, where there was slavery, but it was not a very strong a part of society.

boycott: refusing to buy a product or service to protest the policies of the company selling it.

civil rights: the rights belonging to individuals because they are citizens of a nation.

Confederacy: also called "the South;" another name for the Confederate States of America, the nation formed by the states that had seceded.

constitution: the most basic law of an area, which sets up the structure and powers of the government and the rights of the people.

impeachment: the process in which the House accuses the president of "high crimes and misdemeanors," and the Senate carries out a trial. Two-thirds of the senators must vote guilty for the president to be removed from office.

nonviolent resistance: the practice of using peaceful tactics to gain a political goal.

pardon: legally forgiving someone of a crime.

ratify: to formally approve an amendment to a constitution, putting it into effect.

Reconstruction: the period after the Civil War during which state governments in the South were reformed; also the process of reforming those governments.

reparation: a payment made to someone to make up for a past wrong.

secede: to formally withdraw from an organization or country; "secession" is the act of seceding.

Union: also called "the North;" another name for the United States of America.

Unionist: person who supported the Union during the Civil War.

veto: refuse to sign a bill passed by Congress or state legislatures; this prevents the bill from becoming law.

Further Resources

These books and web sites cover events after the Civil War, including Reconstruction and the civil rights movement:

WEB SITES

www.civilwaralbum.com The Civil War Album includes modern and wartime photos of Civil War sites and maps and virtual tours of the Gettysburg and Champion Hill battles.

www.civil-war.net The Civil War Home Page web site includes a detailed time line, images of war, information on reenactors, and links to many other Civil War topics.

www.homepages.dsu.edu/jankej/civilwar/civilwar.htm This index web site lists numerous articles on a range of Civil War topics, including Reconstruction and reenactors.

sunsite.utk.edu/civil-war/warweb.html The American Civil War web site contains a number of links to resources, including images of wartime, Civil War reenactors, and descriptions of each state during the war.

BOOKS

Clinton, Catherine. *Scholastic Encyclopedia of the Civil War.* New York: Scholastic Books, 1999.

Collier, Christopher. *The Rise of Industry, 1860–1900.* New York: Benchmark Books, 2000.

Dunn, John M. *The Civil Rights Movement (World History).* San Diego, CA: Lucent Books, 1998.

Hakin, Joy. *A History of Us: Reconstructing America (History of Us).* New York: Oxford University Press, 2003.

Hansen, Joyce. *"Bury Me Not in a Land of Slaves:" African Americans in the Time of Reconstruction (Social Studies, Cultures and People).* New York: Franklin Watts, 2000.

Haskins, James. *The Geography of Hope: Black Exodus from the South after Reconstruction.* Brookfield, CT: Twenty-First Century Books, 1999.

King, Wilma. *Children of the Emancipation (Picture the American Past).* Minneapolis, MN: Carolrhoda Books, 2000.

Wormser, Richard. *The Rise and Fall of Jim Crow: The African-American Struggle Against Discrimination, 1865–1954.* New York: St. Martin's Press, 2003.

Index

Page numbers in *italics* indicate maps and diagrams.